To Lily

For everything there is a colour

The LonelyTree Colouring Book
NICHOLAS HALLIDAY

The Lonely Tree has a new friend called ....
Draw a picture of yourself in the box
and write your name here

It was spring in the woodland.

A carpet of bluebells crept over the woodland floor. On the branches above, new leaves had turned the canopy into a blanket of emerald jewels.

As the days grew warmer, the birds who had flown to Africa in the autumn, were returning from their winter holidays.

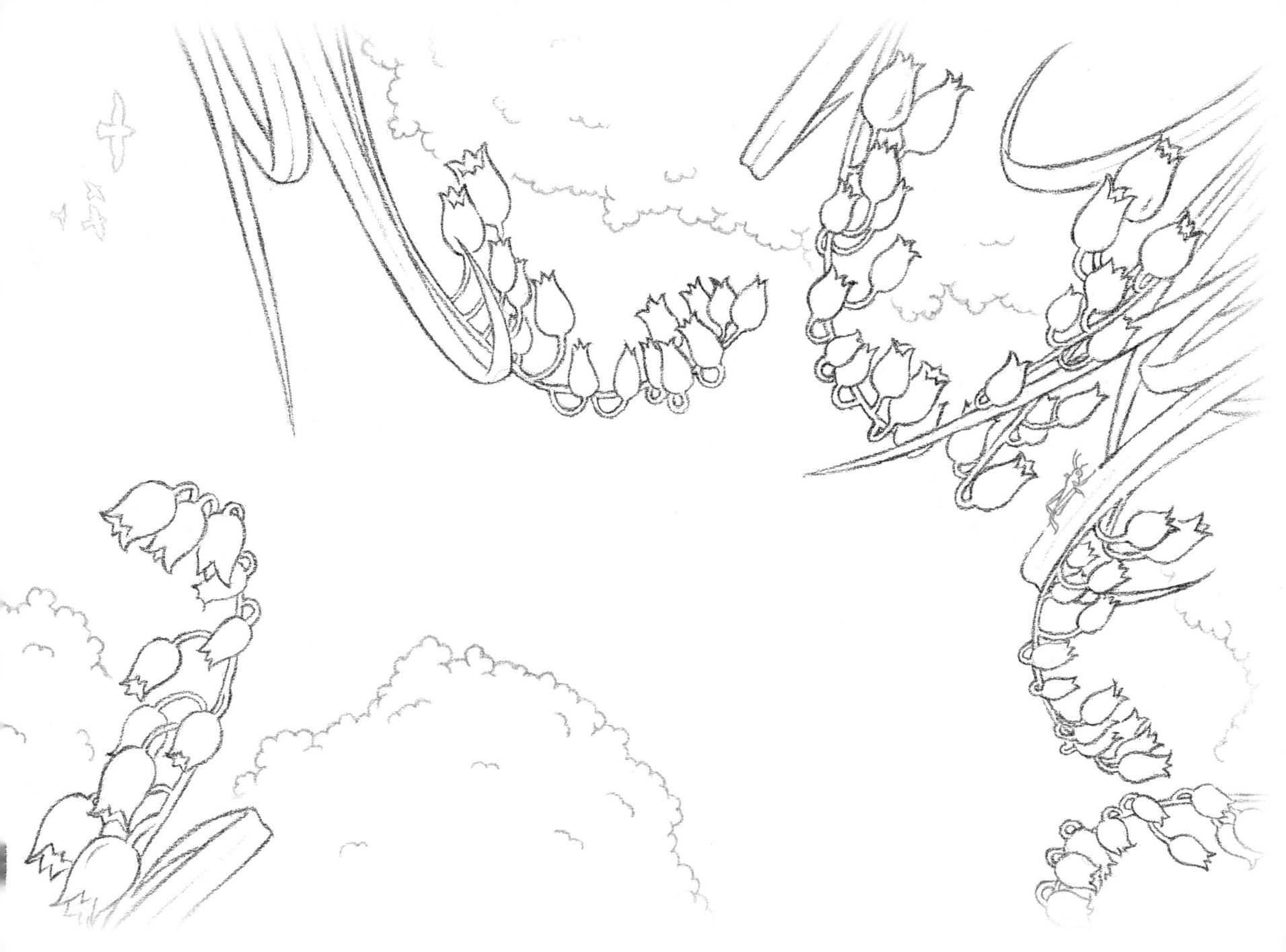

Late one rainy night, something beneath the leaves began to move, sending ripples out through the shallow puddles.

The next morning the woodland woke to an unusual sight.

At the foot of the oldest oak a new tree had begun to grow. No one but the oldest oak had seen anything like it before.

"It certainly isn't like any of us." said the others.

It was summer in the woodland.

The oak greeted the little tree.
"Welcome to the woodland," he said.
"This is your home and we are your friends."

The little tree grew quickly and before long the old oak began telling stories of life in the woodland.

Oak trees can fill a whole summer with stories, but the oldest oak told the best stories of all.

Born long ago, he could remember a time when the woodland was new and dragons still roamed the earth.

All through the summer the little tree listened in wonder and grew taller and stronger every day.

He and the old oak became the best of friends.

It was autumn in the woodland.

One afternoon after listening to a particularly beautiful story, the little tree noticed something.

"Some of your leaves have turned brown," he said to his old friend.
"This happens to all oak trees," his friend replied.
"I am preparing to go to sleep for the winter."
"Will I sleep too?" asked the little tree.
"No," the old oak answered. "You are evergreen, and evergreens never sleep."

Acorns fell with the leaves and covered the ground in deep seasonal colour.

On the last damp evening of autumn, the birds flew away to the warmth of Africa, and the last acorn fell from the old oak.

"I am very tired," he said to his little friend, "I have to sleep now. Always remember that I love you."

It was winter in the woodland.

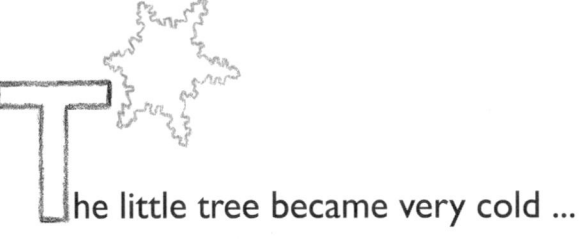

The little tree became very cold ...

... and very lonely.

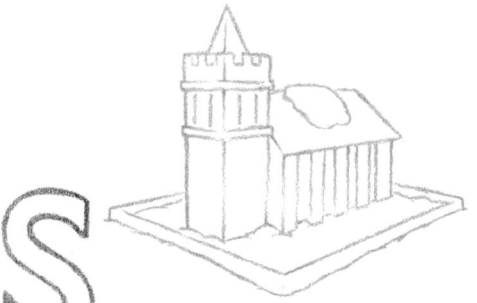

S heets of white snow covered the woodland.

The only winter visitor was a graceful barn owl who perched on top of the old oak on Christmas morning.

"There are bright coloured lights in the town," he called, "and children are singing carols in the churchyard."

As the owl flew away the lonely tree felt lonelier than ever.

One night when the lonely tree thought the winter might never end, a shooting star raced overhead.

As it illuminated the woodland he saw new leaves on the oaks, but the star hurried by so quickly he thought he must have been dreaming.

It was spring in the woodland.

Next morning a wonderful sight greeted the lonely tree.

A carpet of bluebells crept over the woodland floor. On the branches above, new leaves had again turned the canopy into a blanket of emerald jewels.

But something was wrong. There was not a single new leaf on the branches of his old friend.

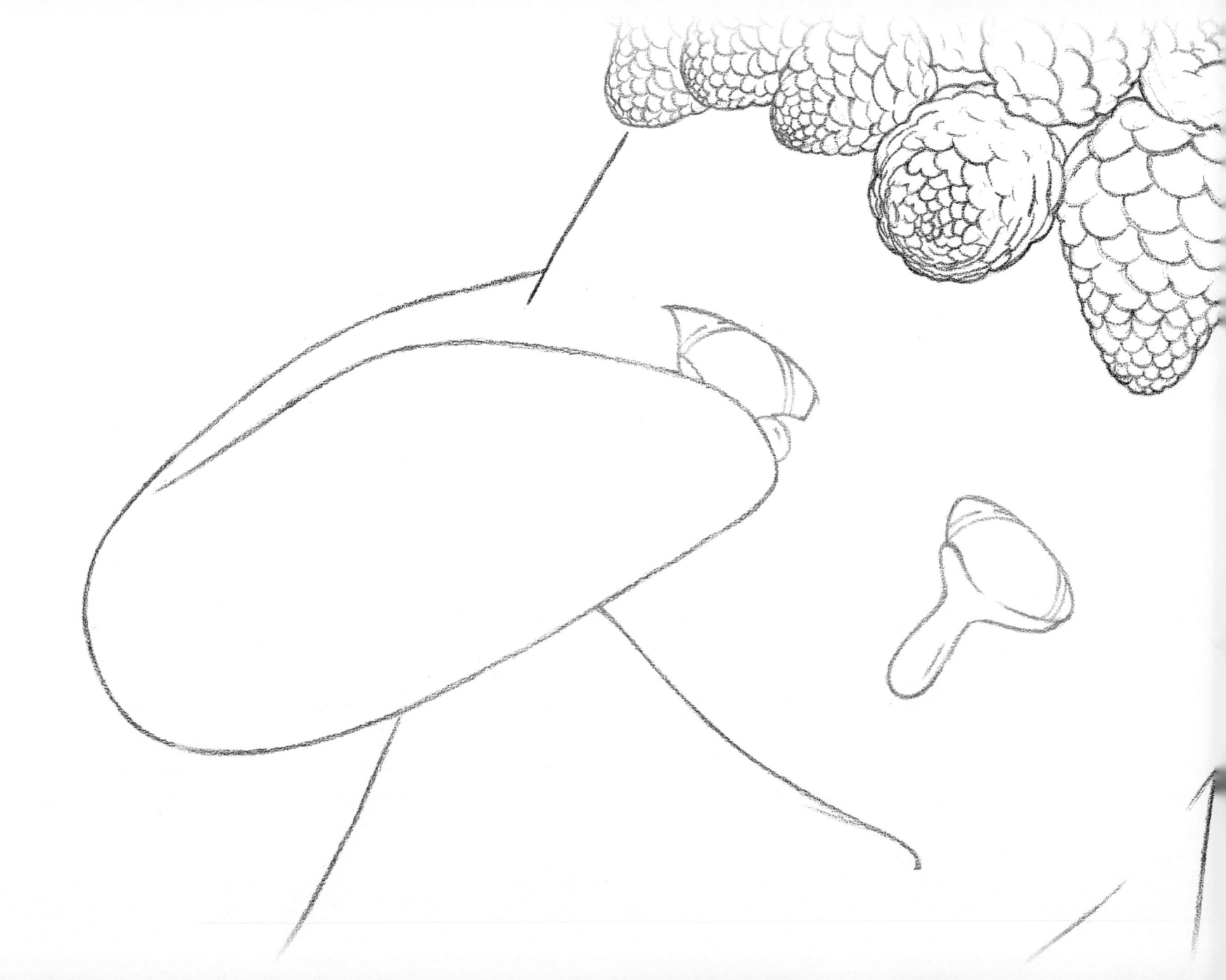

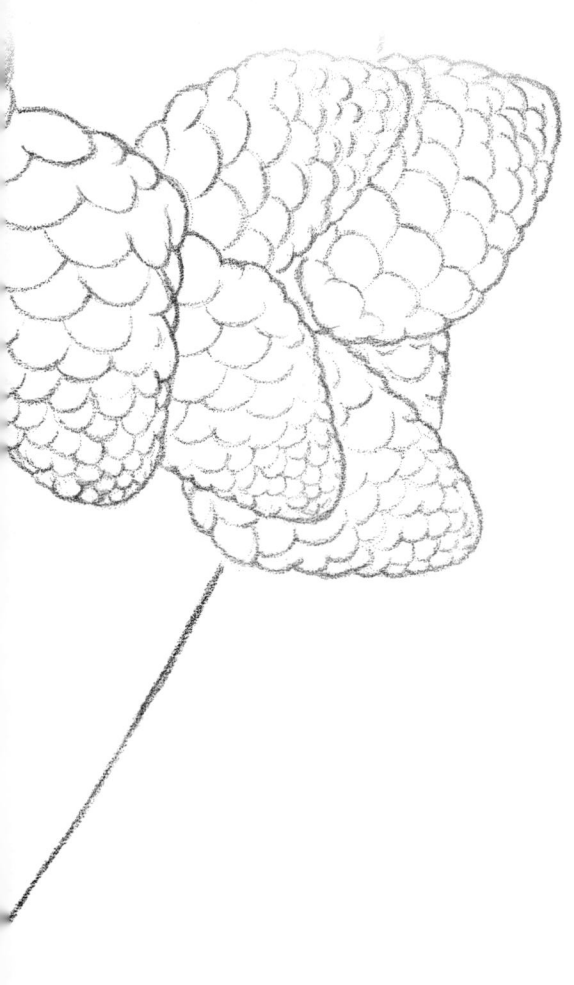

Days passed, and once again the birds returned to the woodland.

"Why is my friend still asleep?" asked the lonely tree.
"His long life has ended," replied the other oaks with sadness. "He has died."

The lonely tree did not understand.

"Death is a part of life," they told him. "He will never wake up, but his love will be with us forever."

The lonely tree now only had memories of his old friend. Memories of his stories, his strength, his wisdom, and most of all, his love.

One late spring day when the lonely tree was feeling especially sad, a miraculous thing happened. In the very place where that last acorn had fallen, a tiny oak tree was beginning to grow.

It was summer in the woodland.

It was the first of many wonderful summers.

The lonely tree greeted the little oak and began retelling stories of life in the woodland.

As they grew, their roots went deeper and deeper into the ground.

Now the lonely tree understood that
for everything there was a season.

Summer brings warmth and the time to grow.
Autumn provides us with seeds for the future.
Without a friend, winter can be cold and lonely,
but spring always brings new life.

The two trees can still be seen in the woodland,
and they are of course, the best of friends.

This colouring book contains hand drawn pencil illustrations based on the original images from *The Lonely Tree*. Universally praised for its simplicity and power, *The Lonely Tree* is now a modern classic.

A portrait of Nicholas Halliday drawn by his daughter Lily in 2002, aged 3 years.

ABOUT THE AUTHOR AND ILLUSTRATOR

NICHOLAS HALLIDAY studied at Epsom School of Art and Design, Lancashire University and Kingston University. Since graduating from Kingston in 1991 with a BA in graphic design, he has worked as an author, illustrator and designer and now runs the independent children's publisher HallidayBooks. He has a daughter Lily, to whom *The Lonely Tree* and this colouring book are dedicated.

....

Written and illustrated by NICHOLAS HALLIDAY

First edition published 2014 • ISBN: 978-0-9560953-4-3

This special edition was created under license exclusively for GreenAcres Woodland Burials • www.greenacreswoodlandburials.co.uk

www.hallidaybooks.com • www.thelonelytree.co.uk

2014 © HallidayBooks

The author has asserted his moral rights • All rights reserved

No part of this publication may be reproduced in any way without prior permission in writing from the publisher

Printed and bound using paper from responsible sources by Broad Link Enterprise Ltd., Hong Kong • FSC C044144

The Lonely Tree is also available in the following formats:

The Lonely Tree GreenAcres Hardback • ISBN: 978-0-9560953-0-5
The Lonely Tree Paperback • ISBN: 978-0-9560959-8-6

'Lovely gift.'
BBC Springwatch

'A delightful story and so relevant.'
Virginia McKenna, OBE.
Founder of the Born Free Foundation

'Richly illustrated and sympathetically explored for younger readers and, of course, that last acorn is the seed for a happy ending.'
Times Education Supplement